A TRUE BOOK™

Farm to Table
Organic Food

ANN O. SQUIRE

Children's Press®
An Imprint of Scholastic Inc.

Library of Congress Cataloging-in-Publication Data
Names: Squire, Ann, author.
Title: Organic food / by Ann O. Squire.
Other titles: True book.
Description: New York, NY : Children's Press, an imprint of Scholastic Inc., 2017. | Series: A true
    book | Includes bibliographical references and index.
Identifiers: LCCN 2016034438| ISBN 9780531229347 (library binding) | ISBN 9780531235539 (pbk.)
Subjects: LCSH: Natural foods—Juvenile literature. | Organic
    farming—Juvenile literature. | Organic gardening—Juvenile literature.
Classification: LCC TX369 .S68 2017 | DDC 641.3/02—dc23
LC record available at https://lccn.loc.gov/2016034438

Front cover: A family with
baskets of fresh produce
Back cover: A bee on a hive

Find the Truth!

Everything you are about to read is true *except* for one of the sentences on this page.

Which one is **TRUE**?

T or F Organic cows must be allowed to graze outdoors at least 300 days a year.

T or F Organic farms can use pesticides to kill off insects and other pests.

Find the answers in this book.

Contents

THE BIG TRUTH!

Understanding Food Labels

Fruits and
vegetables

4

Piglets

Honey

From Farm to Table

Crops

1 Farmers prepare the soil with compost, manure, or other natural fertilizers.

2 Pests may be controlled by adding certain plants beside or among the farm's main crop. Some farmers build bat houses to attract insect-eating bats.

Livestock

1 Animals are raised organically from the time they are born. Animals may receive vaccinations and other medical care.

2 During their life, animals have access to shelter, clean water, and clean, dry bedding.

3 Crops are harvested once they're mature. Then they're packaged and sent to either grocery stores or factories where they're used as ingredients in other products.

4 After harvest, a field is often allowed to "rest." Farmers may use the land as pasture to feed livestock. They may also plant a different kind of plant.

3 Grazing animals, such as cows, sheep, and goats, must have access to pasture for a total of at least 120 days per year.

4 Eggs and milk are gathered regularly and sent to grocery stores or factories. Animals to be used for meat are sent to approved factories for processing and then sale.

CHAPTER 1

Where Does Organic Food Come From?

Millie and her mom were in the produce section of the local supermarket. They were deciding what fruits and vegetables to add to their cart. Standing before a display of melons, Millie noticed something strange. One bin of melons was priced at $1.99 a pound. Another bin that looked exactly the same was marked $3.50 for a pound. Millie asked her mom what the difference was.

Most supermarkets sell both **organic** and nonorganic, or conventional, produce.

What Does It Mean to Be Organic?

Millie's mom told her that the more expensive melons were organic. Millie had never heard that term before. Organic fruits and vegetables are supposed to be better, her mom said. She knew they were grown differently. She had also noticed that organic produce is nearly always more expensive than nonorganic produce. The nonorganic kind is also called conventional produce.

Farms that want to sell their products as organic must be reviewed and approved by the U.S. Department of Agriculture (USDA).

A farmer sprays crops with chemicals.

Organic refers to the way foods are grown or raised. Organic fruits and vegetables have not been treated with human-made **fertilizers** to make them grow bigger. They have not been sprayed with human-made **pesticides** designed to kill insects. Organic fruits and vegetables cannot be treated with radiation, either, which is sometimes used to destroy insect pests. Processed organic foods cannot contain **artificial** preservatives, colors, or flavors.

A scientist inspects genetically modified corn growing at a laboratory.

Organic farmers also cannot grow plants that have been genetically **modified**. Genes are the part of the cell that informs how a plant or animal grows, looks, and behaves. In genetically modified organisms (GMOs), scientists change one or more genes. The change might make a plant grow faster, resist pests, or survive droughts. GMOs are not considered organic. Some people are worried they are potentially harmful, and scientists continue to research their long-term effects.

Organic Meat, Dairy, and Eggs

It's not just fruits and vegetables that are raised organically. The label can also be applied to products that come from animals, including meat, milk and dairy products, honey, and eggs. To qualify as organic, all food given to the animals must be organic. The animals must be allowed access to the outdoors. They also cannot be given **hormones** designed to speed up growth or **antibiotics**.

Pastures where organic cows graze must be kept organically.

Better for the Planet

There are many reasons people choose to farm organically. The biggest one may be that it's better for the planet. Organic farming practices build healthy soil that is free of the chemicals often used in conventional farming. These chemicals run off the land and pollute nearby waters. They can also poison insects, birds, and other animals. Avoiding the use of these chemicals is better for wildlife.

Even small changes in ecosystems such as wetlands can cause serious damage.

Organic Nutrition

Organic fruits and vegetables carry fewer chemicals. Consumption of chemicals is potentially harmful to people's health. In this way, organic food may be safer. However, do organic fruits and vegetables have more nutrients, such as vitamins and minerals? A few studies have found slightly higher levels of various vitamins and minerals in organic produce. But according to this research, the difference is so small that it would not affect your health. Other studies have shown no nutritional differences at all between organic and conventional produce.

Some farmers grow a variety of produce.

CHAPTER 2

Organic Crops

No matter what they are raising, organic farmers try to stay as close to nature as possible. Just like conventional farms, organic farms experience problems such as insect pests, weeds, and poor quality soil. Organic farmers try to solve these problems without using human-made chemicals. The starting point on most farms is the soil. The better and richer the soil is, the better the crops that can be grown.

Rich soil contains many kinds of bacteria and other living things that help plants grow.

Enriching the Soil

Conventional farmers often use synthetic, or human-made, fertilizers to make the soil healthier. Organic farmers use more natural methods. One way is adding **compost**, which consists of decayed waste from organisms, or living things. This includes grass clippings, food waste, or manure from horses, cows, and other animals. Compost adds nutrients to the soil and reduces the need for chemical fertilizers.

Compost must be turned regularly with a shovel or pitchfork.

Farmers sometimes plant cover crops between rows of other crops.

Clover and other crops grown to improve the soil are often called "green manures."

Cover Crops

From time to time, most organic farmers let the soil "rest" by planting a cover crop such as clover. The cover crop protects the surface of the soil from wind and water **erosion**. It adds nutrients when it is worked into the ground at the end of the growing season. Cover crops also crowd out weeds and attract beneficial insects to the area.

With crop rotation, sheep may graze in different fields each year as the fields rest.

Crop Rotation

On conventional farms, farmers often grow the same crop year after year. This practice robs the soil of nutrients, so more fertilizers are needed for crops to thrive. Organic farmers are more likely to rotate their crops. They may grow wheat one year, plant a cover crop the next year, and graze livestock on the field the following year. When crops are rotated like this, the soil stays healthy and rich.

Natural Pest Control

If you've ever grown tomatoes, lettuce, or other food crops, you know that insects enjoy vegetables just as much as people do. Organic farmers do not spray human-made pesticides on their crops, so how do they deal with pests? One way is to attract beneficial insects. They feed on insect pests before the pests have a chance to feed on and destroy the crops.

Insect pests such as moth caterpillars can cause serious harm to crops if not controlled.

Alyssum

Lettuce

Rows of white alyssum flowers run between rows of lettuce.

Farmers attract good insects by placing the right plants by their crops. For example, aphids are tiny insects that eat and destroy lettuce crops. By planting a flower called alyssum alongside lettuce plants, farmers can attract flies that will eat the aphids. Lygus bugs, another pest, love to munch on strawberries. But they like alfalfa even more. By planting alfalfa near their strawberry plants, farmers can lure the bugs away from their cash crop.

Bringing in the Bats

Insect-eating bats can be the best neighbors for organic farmers. By putting up bat houses around the farm, farmers attract these flying mammals. Bats eat a wide variety of insects. One favorite meal is stinkbugs, which feed on tomatoes. Codling moths, another bat food, attack fruit trees. Bats also eat cucumber beetles, which threaten cucumber crops. And a bat can eat a lot, consuming its weight in insects every night!

Understanding Food Labels

When you go to the grocery store, you will see a lot of different labels. What do these labels actually mean?

DAIRY, ORGANIC & NATURAL

McMahon's Farm
WHOLESALE SPECIALTY FOODS

McMahon's Farm
WHOLESALE SPECIALTY FOODS

Cage

Organic label

All Natural label

Cage free label

ORGANIC Produce carrying a "USDA Organic" label were raised on approved organic farms. For other foods, some or all of the ingredients were organically raised. A basic organic label means at least 95 percent of the ingredients are organic. You might also see "Made with organic___" or "Some organic ingredients," which contain fewer organic substances. Labels that say "100% organic" are completely organic.

ALL NATURAL Products that say they're "all natural" contain no human-made ingredients. These foods are not necessarily organic. They may contain GMOs or products from animals treated with hormones or antibiotics.

EGG LABELS Organic or not, egg cartons can carry a variety of labels. "Cage-free" chickens can roam and lay their eggs in a nest. However, they might not ever go outside. "Free-range" chickens don't live in cages either, but they have access to the outdoors. This access may be limited, though. Chickens that are "pasture raised" have access to a much larger outdoor space. There's often a range of natural foods available to them, from worms in the ground to corn feed. When the weather is bad, there is a barn they can enter for shelter.

CHAPTER 3

Organic Livestock

Farmers can raise animals for meat or other food products organically. Such livestock must be fed only organic food. They also must be kept on land that has been certified, or officially proven, organic. In addition, organic farmers must follow the rules prohibiting GMOs and synthetic hormones. Eggs and milk may be sold to factories for use in other products or to supermarkets. Meat must be processed at certified facilities to be sold as organic.

← Some organic farmers keep pigs, using the animals' manure to fertilize their fields.

What Animals Eat

On conventional farms, livestock may eat a feed of mixed corn and soy. Some, but not all, farms also have pastures where livestock can feed. On organic farms, grazing time is required, and the pasture must be kept organic, just like crops. The livestock can also eat grain-based feed made with corn, soy, or other substances. However, the feed has to be organic.

A cowboy watches over a herd of cattle in Brazil.

A veterinarian gives a cow a vaccine against pink eye and rabies.

Treating Sick Animals

Organic farmers cannot use antibiotics to prevent disease among their livestock. However, organic animals can be vaccinated against disease. A vaccination is a shot or other treatment that prevents certain illnesses. If the animals become ill, they are first treated with approved medicines. If these do not work, the farmer must provide antibiotics or other drugs. After treatment, however, the animal can no longer be sold as organic.

Some conventionally raised chickens are kept in cages.

Lifestyles

Organic farms work to take an animal's natural behaviors into account. This reduces stress and keeps the animals healthier. On conventional farms, for example, animals may be kept indoors for much of their lives. There, they have less opportunity to exercise and limited access to fresh air. This causes stress and the animals' health can suffer, just as it would for a human.

On an organic farm, cows and other livestock must be allowed to graze and exercise outdoors. Sometimes weather or climate can limit how much of the year an animal can be outside. Total grazing time for grass-eating animals, such as cows, sheep, and goats, must be at least 120 days a year. Organic livestock must also have access to shade, clean water, fresh air, shelter from bad weather, and clean, dry bedding at all times.

Cows graze in a pasture.

Free-range chickens wander through their crowded indoor pen.

Many people buy organic meat because they believe the animals were treated more **humanely**. However, organic is not the same as humane. Animals on organic farms may still be tied up or kept in small spaces when they are indoors. Chickens may have their beaks clipped to prevent them from pecking at and injuring one another. Such pecking causes serious injury when chickens are kept in confined spaces. The way animals are treated on organic farms depends a lot on the individual farmer.

Organic Honey

Cows and chickens aren't the only organic animals. There are also organic bees, which produce delicious honey. The United States has no official rules that regulate the production of organic honey. However, the government has made some recommendations based on the rules for other organic animals. For example, bees can't receive antibiotics. Also the area where bees forage for food should be free of unapproved chemicals. This can be a challenge. To meet requirements, hives can't be near nonorganic crops, residential areas, industrial areas, or even most government-owned land!

CHAPTER 4

Problems With Going Organic

By now, you may be sold on the idea of eating organic. Staying away from chemical pesticides is better for you and for planet Earth. Organic farming helps the soil, and organically raised animals often have better lives than those raised on conventional farms. But what are the drawbacks to organic food?

 The countries with the most organic farmland are Australia, Argentina, and the United States.

Paying More

As Millie and her mom noticed, organic foods usually cost more than conventional foods. Organic farming is harder work. For example, organic farmers sometimes add compost to the soil, and weed by hand instead of spraying chemicals. Also, without synthetic fertilizers, organic crops may be smaller than those on conventional farms. These extra costs mean consumers pay higher prices. Many people cannot afford them.

Timeline of Organic Farming

1940s

The term *organic farming* becomes popular as a way to describe environmentally friendly farming without chemicals.

1980

The U.S. Department of Agriculture (USDA) releases a study on the benefits of organic farming methods.

Faster Spoilage

Another issue organic foods face is that they may not stay fresh as long as conventional foods. Conventional produce is often treated with wax or other substances to extend its shelf life. Most of these treatments can't be done to organic produce. What's more, the distribution system for organic foods is not as well developed. It may take longer for organic foods to travel from the farm to the market.

1991
The European Union creates rules regarding organic foods.

2002
The United States establishes standards for organic farming. The USDA begins certifying farms as organic.

Too Many Farms

Organic farms cannot produce as much food per acre as conventional farms. If all farms were organic, we would need many more of them to feed everyone. Some experts estimate the United States would need 109 million acres (441,107 square kilometers) more farmland. That's about the size of the state of California. Eating organic may be a good idea in many cases. But it's important to know that all farming, organic or conventional, impacts the environment. ★

A young girl plants a garden.

Staying Safe

Washing your fruits and vegetables helps remove chemicals that were used on the farm. Both organic and conventional farms use pesticides. Both also tend to use them only when necessary. The difference is that conventional farms can use synthetic pesticides. Organic farms, for the most part, only use pesticides that can be found in nature. Common examples include substances taken from chrysanthemums or the Asian neem tree. However, even natural pesticides can be dangerous to consume. Just remember: always wash before you eat!

ORGANIC FOODS AND YOU!

Are you interested in trying out organic foods? Here are a few things you can do.

START SMALL

Because organic foods usually cost more, begin by replacing a few of the foods you buy with organic versions.

BUY LOCAL

You may live near a place that has farm stands or farmers' markets. These are great places to buy produce directly from the farmers. Not only will it help local farmers, but the food will be fresher than what you find in the supermarket. It will also give you a chance to talk to the farmers about their practices. Are they organic? How do they keep the soil healthy? What problems do they experience with pests?

READ LABELS

Pay attention to any labels you see on a product. If there are any you don't understand, ask an adult for help in looking it up.

GROW YOUR OWN

If you have space, try growing organic vegetables at home. You can also talk to your principal and student council about starting a school garden. Tomatoes, squash, and leafy green vegetables are easy to grow in a garden plot or in a container on your porch.

Is Organic Food Worth the Extra Cost?

Organic farming has a lot of benefits. But it is not a perfect system. People who are in favor of going fully organic argue that it's better for the environment and for consumers. People against the switch argue that the food is unaffordable and the difference between organic and conventional food is not worth the cost.

Which side do you agree with? Why?

Yes Organic is worth the cost!

The higher cost of organic food supports better farming practices. **Conventional farms may use hormones, antibiotics, and synthetic chemicals.** These substances can be absorbed by produce or passed on in the meat, milk, or eggs of livestock. Consuming them can damage a person's health. Organic foods avoid these substances. In addition, **organic farming practices are better for the local environment**. Crop rotation and natural pest and weed control help keep the soil healthy. They also don't pollute the air, ground, and water. **Organic farming is better for livestock, too.** Cows, pigs, chickens, and other farm animals are treated more humanely. This can include more space and time outdoors and time outdoors in the sunshine.

No It's not worth it!

Most produce, conventional or organic, has some pesticide residue. Furthermore, **government organizations strictly limit the amount of pesticide that can remain on conventional produce**. Consumers can reduce their exposure by thoroughly washing fruits and vegetables. Organic farms require more space to produce the same amount of food as conventional farms. Organic farms grow about 19 percent less on average. **To meet our needs organically, we'd have to convert more of the world's wild spaces to farmland.**

Finally, **the high cost limits the amount of organic food many people can afford to buy**. Research has shown that conventional foods are as nutritious as organic foods. It is better for your health to eat a wide variety of conventional fruits and vegetables than the limited organic produce you may be able to purchase.

Top five organic products sold in the United States in 2014: Milk, eggs, broiler chickens, lettuce, and apples

Percent of all food sales in the United States that consist of organic products: 5

Percent of Earth's land surface currently used for agriculture: 35

Top five states in organic food purchases in 2014: California, Washington, Pennsylvania, Oregon, and Wisconsin

Number of organic producers worldwide as of 2014: 2.3 million

Number of certified organic operations in the United States as of 2016: More than 21,700

Did you find the truth?

Organic cows must be allowed to graze outdoors at least 300 days a year.

Organic farms can use pesticides to kill off insects and other pests.

Resources

Book

Loh-Hagan, Virginia. *Organic Garden*. Ann Arbor, MI: Cherry Lake Publishing, 2016.

Malnor, Carol L., and Trina L. Hunner. *Molly's Organic Farm*. Nevada City, CA: Dawn Publications, 2012.

Orr, Tamra B. *Organic Farmer*. Ann Arbor, MI: Cherry Lake Publishing, 2010.

Visit this Scholastic Web site for more information about organic food:

★ www.factsfornow.scholastic.com
Enter the keywords **Organic Food**

Important Words

antibiotics (an-ti-bye-AH-tiks) drugs that are used to kill bacteria and to treat infections and diseases

artificial (ahr-tuh-FISH-uhl) made by people rather than existing in nature

compost (KAHM-pohst) a mixture of materials that came from living things, such as rotted leaves, vegetables, or manure, and are added to the soil to make it more productive

erosion (ih-ROH-zhuhn) the wearing away of something by water or wind

fertilizers (FUR-tuh-lize-urz) substances used to improve the soil so plants grow better

hormones (HOR-mohnz) natural substances that are produced in the body and influence the way the body grows or develops

humanely (hyoo-MANE-lee) in a manner that is kind and not cruel

modified (MAH-duh-fyed) changed slightly in order to meet a specific need

organic (or-GAN-ik) grown or made without the use of artificial chemicals

pesticides (PES-ti-sidez) chemicals used to kill pests such as insects

Index

Page numbers in **bold** indicate illustrations.

About the Author

Ann O. Squire is a psychologist and an animal behaviorist. Before becoming a writer, she studied the behavior of rats, tropical fish in the Caribbean, and electric fish from central Africa. Her favorite part of being a writer is the chance to learn as much as she can about all sorts of topics. In addition to *Organic Foods* and other books in the Farm to Table series, Dr. Squire has written about many different animals, from lemmings to leopards and cicadas to cheetahs. She lives in Asheville, North Carolina.